Contents

Disaster at Sea

Sea travel is as old as history itself. The sea floor is littered with wrecks, big and small, ancient and modern, famous and forgotten. When heading out to sea, captain and crew have responsibility for both their ship and their passengers. They are aware of the hazards they face – storms, icebergs and fog being among the most common. Modern technology has reduced the risk of a ship falling victim to these natural hazards, but human error and negligence are just as much to blame now as they were in the past.

WEATHER HAZARDS

Hurricanes in the Atlantic and typhoons in the Pacific cause severe conditions for ships on the open seas. Navigating a ship to safety and calmer waters through huge waves and high winds requires excellent seamanship. However, modern weather forecasting and ship-to-shore communication mean that, normally speaking, ships should be able to avoid such a situation.

Severe storms are one of the most common hazards facing ships at sea.

FOG

Sailing in thick fog conceals coastlines, reefs, icebergs and other ships. Special navigation tools, such as radar, sonar and global positioning systems all help a ship's crew to navigate when blinded by fog. Ship-to-ship communication helps to avoid collisions.

CATASTROPHE!

SHIPWRECK DISASTERS

John Hawkins

W

This paperback edition published in 2014 by Franklin Watts

Copyright © 2012 Arcturus Publishing Limited

Franklin Watts
338 Euston Road
London NW1 3BH

Franklin Watts Australia
Level 17/207 Kent Street, Sydney NSW 2000

Produced by Arcturus Publishing Limited,
26/27 Bickels Yard, 151–153 Bermondsey Street, London SE1 3HA

Text: John Hawkins
Editors: Joe Harris and Penny Worms
Design: Graham Rich
Cover design: Graham Rich

Picture credits:
Corbis: cover, 7, 15, 20, 29, 31, 39, 44t, 45tc, 45c, 45b. Getty: 1, 8b, 9, 10, 11l, 12, 13, 17, 18, 23, 26b, 27, 33, 34, 37, 44tc, 44c, 44bc, 44b, 45t, 47. Shutterstock: 4, 5, 6, 8t, 11r, 14, 16, 22, 24t, 26t, 28, 30, 32, 36, 38, 40, 42. Wikimedia: 24b, 25, 41, 45bc.
Cover image: Off the coast of Galicia, Spain. The oil tanker Prestige sank with nearly 70,000 tonnes of oil onboard. When it capsized on 13 November 2002, it caused an ecological catastrophe.

A CIP catalogue record for this book is available from the British Library.

Dewey Decimal Classification Number 363.1'23

ISBN 978 1 4451 3132 0

Printed in China

Franklin Watts is a division of Hachette Children's Books, an Hachette UK company.
www.hachette.co.uk

SL001928UK
Supplier 03, Date 0114, Print Run 3212

A shipwreck on the seabed soon turns into a vibrant marine habitat.

HUMAN ERROR

Overcrowding, lack of judgement, or poor maintenance have caused some of the worst ferry disasters.

Sometimes, a lack of safety equipment or lifeboats has contributed to the huge losses of life.

 ## SEARCH AND RESCUE

The fate of the survivors of a shipwreck is often sealed by the speed at which the alarm is raised and how quickly help can get to the scene. It is the unwritten law of the sea that if a ship sends an SOS signal, any nearby ships have a duty to respond. Bad weather conditions can hamper rescue efforts and that is when air-sea rescue helicopters become vital.

MV *Princess of the Stars*, 2008

The *Princess of the Stars* was a Philippine passenger ferry on her way from the country's capital, Manila, to Cebu City. She left port on the morning of 21 June 2008 with 845 people on board despite typhoon warnings. In the midst of the storm, she capsized. Those who jumped into the stormy water stood as little chance as those trapped below deck.

THE *PRINCESS*

The *Princess of the Stars* was a large and relatively modern ship owned by Sulpicio Lines, the biggest ferry operator in the Philippines. Sulpicio had a terrible track record but the *Princess* had the company's most experienced captain at the helm.

TYPHOON FENGSHEN

The Philippines suffer tropical storms and typhoons every year. Typhoon Fengshen (or Frank) was the second that year to directly hit the Islands. Sulpicio claims that, at the time the *Princess* set sail, the storm warning was not severe enough to prevent a ship that large from leaving port.

HIGH WAVES

Strong winds started to rock the *Princess*. At 9 am the crew told the passengers to put on life jackets. By noon, the rocking was so severe that some passengers started to jump or fall off the boat. The coast guard lost radio contact at 12.30 pm. When rescuers reached the capsized ship almost 24 hours later, only the tip of her hull was visible. Only 52 people survived.

Grieving relatives attend a mass at the site of the capsized ferry. Shortly afterwards, divers resumed their efforts to retrieve bodies.

INQUIRY

A marine inquiry concluded that the cause of the capsizing 'was the failure of the Master to exercise extraordinary diligence and good seamanship thereby committing an error of judgment that brought [the *Princess*] in harm's way into the eye of Typhoon Fengshen (Frank).' The captain's body was never found, along with almost 500 other victims.

LEARNING FROM CATASTROPHES

After the disaster, the Philippine Coast Guard issued new guidelines for stormy weather. Only vessels over 907 tonnes should sail when the Public Storm Warning Signal is at 1, its lowest level. Above that, no vessels should sail unless to seek shelter and they should not carry passengers. In 2010, the president supported the funding of new rescue helicopters, the lack of which had added to the high death toll of the *Princess* disaster.

RMS *Titanic*, 1912

At the beginning of the 20th century, before air travel took over, huge numbers of people travelled between Europe and North America by ship. Shipping companies were in competition to make the fastest crossing and to provide passengers with the most luxurious surroundings. No ship was bigger, faster or finer than the *Titanic*. Her reign as the supreme cruise liner was tragically cut short.

The Titanic sets off on her maiden voyage from Southampton.

WHITE STAR LINE

In 1899, the White Star Line brought the *Oceanic* into service. The *Oceanic* had luxury cabins with private bathrooms and electric bells to summon the stewards. When Bruce Ismay took over the company, he wanted to go one better.

A NEW GENERATION

With the Belfast shipbuilder Harland & Wolff, Ismay set about building a new generation of luxury liners. One of them was the *Titanic*. When she set off on her maiden voyage from Southampton to New York on 10 April 1912, she was the largest and most luxurious ship afloat. Her

This portrait shows Captain Edward J Smith.

funnels were as big as train tunnels and her propellers were the size of windmills.

LUXURY CRUISING

The *Titanic* had nine decks that could accommodate 3,547 people – 905 in first class, 564 in second class and 1,134 in third class. The other 944 on board were crew. The best suites cost £870 one way – more than £60,000 in today's money. The *Titanic* was one of the first ships to have a swimming pool.

EYEWITNESS

Eva Hart was seven years old when she travelled with her family on board the *Titanic*. They had been transferred from another ship. In a recording in 1987, she said: 'I was excited because my father was so delighted about it. My mother was horrified. My mother said to my father, "Isn't that the ship that they say is unsinkable?" And he said, "No. It's the ship that is unsinkable." I clearly remember the look on her face.' It seemed as though her mother had had a premonition.

UNSINKABLE

The *Titanic* was thought to be unsinkable because she had a double hull made of iron. The outer skin was 2.5 cm (1 inch) thick. It was divided into 16 watertight compartments. Four of these could be flooded without endangering the ship's buoyancy.

The *Titanic* *had nine decks accommodating 3,547 people.*

FIRST CLASS GUESTS

There were 2,224 people on board for the maiden voyage. These included John Jacob Astor – reputedly the richest man in the world – with his young wife, and Mr and Mrs Straus, the owners of Macy's, then the world's largest department store. The owner Bruce Ismay was also on board and the ship was commanded by Captain Edward J Smith. This was planned to be his last voyage. He was retiring after being with the White Star Line for 38 years.

WARNINGS

The *Titanic* was taking a northerly route in the hope of making a faster passage. But it was April and very cold. The sea was very still and there was a slight mist with no moonlight. The ship had received warnings of icebergs and ice fields but was still travelling at about 20 knots.

ICEBERG!

At 11.40 pm the lookout, Fred Fleet, in the crow's nest, saw an iceberg. He sounded the alarm and, in trying to avoid a collision, the *Titanic* turned hard to starboard (right). It was too late. The *Titanic* struck the iceberg on the starboard side, shaving off ice, which landed on the forward deck. Survivors described it more as a series of three bumps rather than a glancing blow and then the *Titanic* came to a grinding halt.

WHY DID IT HAPPEN?

Below the waterline, the iceberg had caused a huge gash. The watertight compartments began to fill. Then a fault in the design became apparent. The walls of the watertight compartments did not extend all the way to the deck above and, as one filled, the water spilled over into the next. Twenty minutes after the collision, five compartments were filled and it was clear that the *Titanic* was going down.

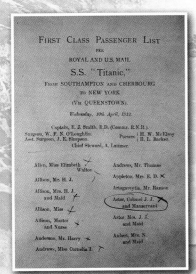

This is the opening page of the first class passenger list. First class passengers paid £870 for the very best suites.

MAN THE LIFEBOATS

At 12.30 am, Captain Smith gave the order to man the lifeboats. However, there were only 16 wooden lifeboats and four collapsible life rafts. There was enough room for just 1,178 of the 2,224 people on board. Women and children were to go first. By 2 am all the lifeboats had left. In the confusion, not all of them were full and 1,500 people remained on board. Some leapt into the icy waters, while others huddled together on the stern.

GOING DOWN

Those in the lifeboats watched as water flooded the forward compartments and then the hull snapped between the third and fourth funnels. The stern of the ship rose up completely out of the water. It took 2 hours and 40 minutes for the great ship to sink.

RESCUE

The liner *Californian* was less than 32 km (20 miles) away, but its wireless operator was not on duty that night. Another ship, the *Carpathia*, heard the *Titanic*'s distress calls and raced to the rescue, arriving 1 hour and 20 minutes after she had gone down. The *Carpathia* picked up 705 people. However, 1,519 lost their lives, many dying from hypothermia in the freezing waters.

FINDING THE *TITANIC*

In September 1985, after many years of searching, the wreck of the *Titanic* was finally located by a joint French and American team, using underwater video cameras. The ship lies in two pieces, 4 km (2.5 miles) down and 640 km (400 miles) off Canada's Newfoundland coast.

There were lifeboats and rafts for just 1,178 of the 2,224 people on board.

LEARNING FROM CATASTROPHES

Following the disaster the first International Convention for Safety of Life at Sea was called in London. Under its rules, all ships had to carry enough lifeboats for all those on board. Ships had to maintain a 24-hour radio watch and an International Ice Patrol was set up to warn of icebergs in the North Atlantic shipping lanes.

DAILY GRAPHIC
ACCIDENT £1,000 INSURANCE
TUESDAY, APRIL 16, 1912
TITANIC SUNK: APPALLING LOSS OF LIFE

EGYPT

SAUDI ARABIA

RED SEA

MV *Al-Salam Boccaccio 98*, 2006

The *Al-Salam Boccaccio 98* was a ferry carrying an estimated 1,400 passengers and crew across the Red Sea from Saudi Arabia to Egypt. It sank 70 km (43 miles) off the coast of Egypt at approximately 2 am on 3 February 2006, killing more than 1,000 people.

PASSENGERS

Most of the passengers were either Egyptians working in Saudi Arabia or pilgrims who had been to the Islamic holy city of Mecca. There were also a few hundred vehicles on the vehicle decks below.

FIRE ON BOARD

Engineering student Isra Ibrahim Abdul-Rahman told his story to the *Washington Post*. He said he smelled oily smoke but was reassured by a crew member that there was a small fire below and they were taking care of it. At 1 am, he saw black smoke billowing out of the vehicle deck and the ship started to list (lean) badly. In minutes, the ship capsized. There was no SOS. Ten big lifeboats that could carry 100 passengers each were never lowered.

BREAKING NEWS

Distraught relatives ransacked the offices of the ferry operators, desperate for news of their family members. Reports in the newspapers from survivors fuelled their anger because it appeared that the fire had started just one hour from the Saudi port of Duma. No one knows why the captain did not turn the ferry back. He perished with his ship.

According to records, there was enough life-saving equipment for about three times the number of passengers.

RESCUE

Only 388 people survived the disaster, many in inflatable rafts activated by anyone who knew how they worked. Some clung to life rings for more than 20 hours before they were fished from the water.

 ## POSSIBLE CAUSES

It seems that crew members tackling the fire down below were using water pumped up from the sea. The fire kept restarting and the seawater did not drain. One crew member said, 'Drains were blocked by cargo. The ship was filling up.' All the water on the vehicle deck made the ship much less stable.

SS *Mont Blanc*, 1917

On 6 December 1917, the Norwegian vessel SS *Imo* ran into the **SS *Mont Blanc*,** a French freighter in the harbour of Halifax, Nova Scotia. The *Mont Blanc* was loaded with 4,500 tonnes of explosives. The collision caused a colossal explosion that killed 1,635 people.

IT'S WAR

As World War I was raging in Europe (1914–18), Halifax became Canada's major wartime port. Here troops and supplies were loaded onto ships for the perilous journey across the Atlantic to Europe. In December 1917, the port was full of ships, including the SS *Imo*.

SS *IMO*

The SS *Imo* was a supply vessel. She was on her way to New York to load relief supplies for Belgium and had a huge sign saying 'Belgian Relief' on her sides. This was to show her neutrality to any German U-boats lurking out in the Atlantic.

MONT BLANC

The previous evening, the *Mont Blanc* had arrived from New York too late to enter the harbour. The anti-submarine nets had been raised so she had to wait until the next morning. She was carrying highly explosive material – 2,000 tonnes of picric acid, used for making artillery shells; 180 tonnes of TNT; 9 tonnes of gun cotton; and she had drums of Benzol (a high-octane fuel) stacked on her decks.

Halifax was Canada's major wartime port.

COLLISION COURSE

On the morning of 6 December 1917, the *Imo* weighed anchor and headed for the sea, just as the *Mont Blanc* was entering the harbour. They collided in the bottleneck known as the 'Narrows'. Some of the Benzol drums broke loose and spilled on the deck. They caught fire and Captain Le Medec, knowing how dangerous their cargo was, ordered all hands to abandon ship. So, unmanned and on fire, the *Mont Blanc* drifted towards the harbour.

WHY DID IT HAPPEN?

As both ships entered the Narrows, *Imo* was on the wrong side, having moved over for an earlier ship. A series of confusing whistle signals put them on a collision course. *Mont Blanc* steered hard to port (left) and *Imo* reversed its engines to stop.

However, this made *Imo* swing into *Mont Blanc*'s path. The captain and pilot of *Mont Blanc* were charged with manslaughter. The charges were dropped when the Supreme Court of Canada judged that both ships were at fault.

EXPLOSION!

At around 9.05 am, the *Mont Blanc* blew up. The whole ship disintegrated in a massive explosion that killed more than 1,500 people instantly. It was the biggest man-made explosion ever known until the atomic bomb.

The wreck of the freighter SS Imo *in Halifax harbour, 7 December 1917.*

DEVASTATION

The blast flattened the buildings for 5 square km (2 square miles). In all, an area of 132 ha (325 acres) was devastated and most of the windows in Halifax were blown out. Many who had rushed to see what had happened suffered eye injuries from the flying glass. Many others suffered burns and other injuries.

MUSHROOM CLOUD

A mushroom-shaped cloud rose several miles into the sky, and 2,700 tonnes of metal rained down on Halifax. The ship's gun was thrown a distance of 2.4 km (1.5 miles), while part of an anchor landed in woods some 5 km (3 miles) away.

TSUNAMI AND FIRE

The blast caused a man-made tsunami – a wave that was so high that it overwhelmed some smaller vessels. Fires raged and threatened the naval weapons store at the Wellington Barracks. The area was evacuated and the weapons store was made safe by dumping its contents into the harbour. Rescuers rushed to the city but their job was made harder by nightfall and the beginning of a terrible blizzard.

LASTING LEGACY

The port of Halifax was put out of operation, which had a devastating effect on the war effort. Funds poured in from around the world, but most of the relief came from the state of Massachusetts. Now, every year Halifax presents Boston with a giant Christmas tree to show its gratitude.

EYEWITNESS

Peggy Gregoire was about nine when it happened. She went to St Patrick's Girls' School, a Catholic school run by nuns. 'When the explosion came, the sister was standing at the window, with the back of her head toward the glass. At that time, [the nuns] wore a little leather cap, quite close around the neck. When the explosion happened, she came up to the front of the room, and just warned us it was fire drill – no talking. And there was blood coming down from her little cap. We were all terrified.'

PORTSMOUTH

Mary Rose, 1545

On the evening of 19 July 1545, King Henry VIII watched from the shore as his flagship, the *Mary Rose*, led the English fleet out of Portsmouth harbour to engage the attacking French fleet. On board were 185 soldiers, 200 seamen and 30 gunners. Most of them never returned.

This oil painting depicts the sinking of the Mary Rose.

GUNS ON THE LOOSE

The *Mary Rose* was the fastest ship in the fleet. She quickly outran the other British ships. When she came under fire from the French warships, she put about to fire a broadside and wait for support. A gust of wind caught her as she turned, causing her to heel (tilt) over. It is widely believed that her newly installed deck guns broke loose and crashed into her leeward side, unbalancing the ship. Her lower gun ports were open so, as she tipped, they dropped below the water level and the ship quickly filled with water.

SINKING SHIP

The *Mary Rose* sank and most of the crew drowned because they became caught in the netting set up to stop the enemy from boarding. Only a handful working high in the rigging survived.

OUTDATED

At the time of her loss the *Mary Rose* was already outdated. Built in 1510, she had been modified several times to carry different weapons. By 1545, she was too cumbersome and slow to meet the challenge of the French galleys, which were easy to manoeuvre because they were powered by oarsmen and not the wind. The mixed battery of medium- and short-range weapons was hard to combine effectively, and this type of ship became too small to carry enough good sailors as well as soldiers.

A NEW WARSHIP

Henry VIII had already developed a new type of ship, armed with heavy guns and better sailors. It was a development of his new ships that his daughter Elizabeth I used to defeat the Spanish Armada in 1588.

RAISING THE *MARY ROSE*

Early attempts to raise the *Mary Rose* just days after the sinking failed, although some of her guns were recovered. The site was then lost and work only began again in the 1970s.

After a major survey of the area, the *Mary Rose* was lifted in two halves in 1982. She is conserved in Portsmouth, along with over 22,000 artefacts that were found on board.

NANTUCKET

Andrea Doria, 1956

At 11 pm on 26 July 1956, the Swedish cruise ship *Stockholm* sliced through the fog off Nantucket and into the side of the Italian passenger ship *Andrea Doria*. After struggling to stay afloat for 12 hours, the crippled Italian liner sank in the worst liner collision in history.

UNSINKABLE

Despite the fate of the *Titanic*, the *Andrea Doria* was thought to be unsinkable. Built with the most modern technology available, she had all the newest safety equipment. In just three years, she had crossed the Atlantic a hundred times and was scheduled to arrive in New York's harbour the following morning.

COLLISION

Both ships were equipped with radar. However, officers made miscalculations in the thick fog. The two ships were travelling at full speed when they collided. The Swedish ship had a reinforced, ice-breaking bow, which struck the Italian passenger liner on her starboard side.

DOOMED

As the *Stockholm* reversed her engines to pull her bow out of the Italian liner's side, she made more holes along the side of the *Andrea Doria*. It soon became clear that the Italian ship was doomed.

The Andrea Doria *sinks, taking 51 people down with her.*

LIFEBOATS

Because she was listing so badly on her starboard side, it made most of the lifeboats useless. Those along the port side lay against the side of the ship and could not be lowered. Those on the starboard side were hanging too far from the ship for passengers to step into them.

RESCUE

An SOS signal brought many ships, led by the French liner *Ile de France*. Eventually the starboard lifeboats were lowered into the sea and ropes were rigged to lower passengers into them. The *Ile de France* sent its own lifeboats and picked up 753 survivors. Others rowed over to the badly damaged *Stockholm*. In all 51 people died, while 1,600 were rescued.

EYEWITNESS

Miss Joan Dier was on the *Andrea Doria*. In 1975, she told the *Buffalo Evening News*: 'The decks were very crowded and people were bumping into each other. I could see many persons bleeding and limping from the injuries they had received.'

Some people formed a chain, helping passengers to the ropes so they could climb down into the boats. Joan said, 'As the boat moved away, I looked at the *Andrea Doria* on her side. It was like she was sleeping under a starry sky.'

SS *Eastland*, 1915

At 7.28 am on 24 July 1915, the excursion steamer *Eastland* slowly rolled over while she was still moored to her dock on the south bank of the Chicago River. There were 2,572 passengers on board, and 844 of them died. This was the most terrible disaster in Chicago's history.

ON BOARD

The steamer was largely carrying Western Electric employees and their families, going to an annual company picnic in Michigan City, Indiana. A day such as this caused much excitement.

UNSTABLE

The causes of the disaster are still subject to debate, but several facts are clear. The *Eastland* had a reputation for being top-heavy. There had been reports of her listing in an alarming way previously. The ship had a water-ballasting system, which meant that the crew could let water into its ballast tanks to stabilize the ship. However, many people said this was not enough.

A journey on the Eastland *should have been a treat for the passengers, many of whom were too poor to take vacations.*

LIFEBOATS

Following the *Titanic* disaster, an act had been passed that meant the *Eastland* had to have more lifeboats fitted, adding even more weight. She tipped over the first time there was a full passenger load after this change was made. Ironically, the fatal addition was those extra lifeboats.

Those lucky enough walked off the side of the Eastland *into waiting tugs. Many more were trapped inside.*

HUMAN TRAGEDY

Those on the starboard side of the steamer were the lucky ones. As the *Eastland* tipped over port side, those on the starboard side could climb over the railing onto the side of the hull. Those people inside were trapped. All those on the port side fell into the river, followed by deck furniture and then more people. Some made it to the shore but many drowned in the chaos.

AFTERWARDS

Lawsuits continued for more than 20 years. The *Eastland* herself was repaired, renamed the *Wilmette*, and became a naval training vessel until she was broken up for scrap in 1947.

 EYEWITNESS

One eyewitness described the scene: 'I shall never be able to forget what I saw. People were struggling in the water, clustered so thickly that they literally covered the surface of the river. A few were swimming; the rest floundered about, clutching at anything that they could reach – screaming. The screaming was the most horrible of all.'

SS *Empress of Ireland*, 1914

At around 2 am on 29 May 1914, a tragedy on a similar scale to the *Titanic* occurred in thick fog in the St Lawrence River in Canada. It involved the large transatlantic steamship, *Empress of Ireland*, and a Norwegian coal ship, the *Storstad*.

FIRST SIGHTING

The *Empress of Ireland* was bound from Quebec City to Liverpool. That night, Captain Henry Kendall spotted the mast lights of the *Storstad* approaching in the distance before thick fog rolled in. Ironically, if Kendall had continued on his course the two ships would have passed without incident, but he was a cautious man.

EVASIVE ACTION

Kendall put all engines into reverse, slowing the ship. He sounded the ship's horn three times warning other traffic of his presence and the *Empress of Ireland* and the *Storstad* exchanged warning signals in the fog. Then suddenly, without warning, the lights of the *Storstad* reappeared less than 9 m (10 yards) away.

The Empress of Ireland *was struck and sunk by the Norwegian coal ship* Storstad.

IMPACT

Using a megaphone, he shouted to the commander of the *Storstad* to throw his vessel into reverse while he turned to port to minimize the impact. The *Storstad* was still travelling at 10 knots when she struck the *Empress* on her starboard side. Water poured in so quickly that people sleeping in the starboard cabins stood no chance.

The Empress of Ireland *sank just 14 minutes after the initial collision.*

FULL STEAM AHEAD

With the ship listing heavily, Captain Kendall ordered full speed ahead in an attempt to run the *Empress* aground. Then the engines suddenly broke down. All the lights went out. Five or six lifeboats were launched successfully. Those who could find their way to the side in the darkness threw themselves into the freezing water.

DEATH TOLL

Just 14 minutes after the collision, the *Empress of Ireland* sank. Of the 1,477 on board, 1,012 lost their lives, including 840 passengers – eight more passengers than had died in the *Titanic* disaster.

WHY DID IT HAPPEN?

One of the reasons the *Empress* sank so quickly was that many portholes had been left open. Normally the rule is that all portholes should be closed once a voyage is underway. Because the *Empress*'s list was so extreme, water simply poured in, and this made the list even worse.

MV *Doña Paz*, 1987

In the early hours of 21 December 1987, the Philippine ferry *Doña Paz* was bound from Leyte island to the capital, Manila, when it collided with an oil tanker, the *Vector*. There is some debate over how many people were on board, but it could have been as many as 4,000, making this the worst ferry disaster in history.

OVERCROWDED

Ferries are a common form of transportation in the Philippines, an archipelago of about 7,000 islands. The *Doña Paz* ferried people between Manila and other islands twice a week. It was only supposed to carry 1,518 people, but over the Christmas period, many more were on board. Most were families with children, who were not on the roster.

INFERNO

The *Vector* was a Philippine tanker carrying more than 8,000 barrels of gasoline and kerosene. On impact, the cargo burst into flames, setting both ships and the surrounding sea on fire. Some able swimmers swam underneath the flames to clear waters. Many were burned alive in the ship or in the water.

RESCUE

Only 24 people survived the accident. They were in the water for over an hour before help arrived in the form of a passing ship, the *Don Claudio*. By that time, both the *Doña Paz* and the *Vector* had sunk.

Relatives search a hastily posted survivors' list for news of their loved ones.

AFTERMATH

Sulpicio Lines, owners of the *Doña Paz*, quickly offered money to the victims' families, but only to those on the ship's roster. However, a Board of Inquiry ruled that the *Vector* was at fault. She was not seaworthy, and did not have enough crew.

 EYEWITNESS

Aludia Bacsal was only 18 years old. She was excited to be going to the capital for Christmas with her father, Salvadore. She said, 'There were so many people. We were like cockroaches or ants. People were getting restless. It was very noisy.' That night, Salvadore saw the approaching *Vector* and knew they were going to crash. After the impact, he said, 'I ran back to my daughter and told her there was a fire. I told her we were going to jump overboard.' They did not know the sea they were jumping into was also on fire. Aludia was badly burned but they both survived.

STOCKHOLM

TALLINN

MV *Estonia*, 1994

The MV *Estonia* was a roll-on, roll-off (ro-ro) car ferry bound for Stockholm carrying 989 passengers. As she set sail from Tallinn, Estonia, on the evening of 27 September 1994, the weather started to deteriorate. Shortly after midnight, conditions were rough enough to force the ship's band to stop playing. An hour later, there was a loud bang and the ferry started to sink.

TROUBLE ON BOARD

The first bang seemed to come from the bow-door area. It is thought that this was when the locks on the huge steel bow door were damaged. At around 1.15 am, the bow door broke off completely. An investigation later found that the door snagged the inner ramp as it flew off, leaving the hull open to the waves.

TAKING IN WATER

Tonnes of water cascaded in through the open hull and the Estonia began to list heavily to starboard. No alarm was raised. However, passengers were already struggling to get on deck via the stairways, which were now at a crazy angle. At 1.22 am the first SOS was sent from the *Estonia*.

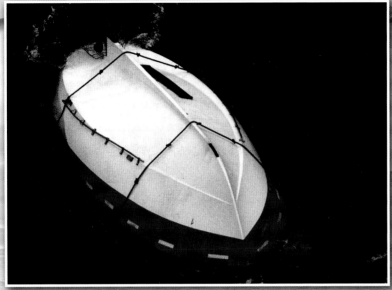

This lifeboat from the Estonia capsized and so was useless to those in the freezing water.

ON DECK

On deck, some passengers and crew struggled to find life jackets and launch life rafts. Others clung to the hull, believing a ship as big as the *Estonia* would not sink. Tragically, they were wrong. At roughly 1.50 am, the *Estonia*'s bow reared upward and she slipped beneath the Baltic Sea. The screams from passengers still trapped inside fell silent.

RESCUE EFFORT

Although a passenger ferry arrived shortly afterwards, the weather conditions were so bad that the crew struggled to rescue anyone. Those in the water were dead by the time the first helicopters arrived, at around 3 am. The helicopters attempted to winch up a life raft but the cables snapped. Finally, at around 9 am, the remaining 138 survivors were winched to safety. One died later in hospital.

WHY DID IT HAPPEN?

The official report of the Joint Accident Investigation Commission of Estonia, Finland and Sweden concluded that the *Estonia*'s builders were at fault. Nevertheless, the report did not clear the crew and officers on board that night of negligence.

MEMPHIS

SS *Sultana*, 1865

At 2 am on 27 April 1865, the huge paddlewheel steamer *Sultana* sank on the Mississippi River. Some 1,547 died – exceeding the death toll of the *Titanic*. However, few people have heard of the sinking of the *Sultana* because other events overshadowed the story.

WAR MISSION

The *Sultana* was launched two years before the American Civil War (1861–65). The Union (the northern states) used her to be able to carry troops and supplies up and down the Ohio, Missouri and Mississippi rivers. When the war ended, the *Sultana* was sailed to Vicksburg, Mississippi, to take Union troops who had been held prisoner in the south, back home to the north.

OVERLOADED

The *Sultana*'s capacity was just 376, but on that fateful trip she was carrying nearly 2,100 former prisoners-of-war, many so weak they had to be carried on board on stretchers. They were escorted by 22 soldiers. There were also 90 paying passengers and a crew of 88. In the cargo holds were 2,000 barrels of sugar and a large alligator in a crate, which the captain had bought in New Orleans as a mascot. Some people expressed concern that the ship was being overloaded when they saw crew wedging large beams under the decks. The decks were sagging under the weight of passengers.

The Sultana *was loaded with 2,200 people, 60 horses, a cargo of sugar and an alligator!*

BOILER TROUBLE

The *Sultana's* journey was delayed slightly when it developed a bulge and leak in one of its four boilers. Engineers advised the captain to have two boiler plates removed and replaced, but the captain refused. Instead he made do by riveting a metal patch over the problem area.

 WHY DID IT HAPPEN?

The *Sultana* was skippered by maverick captain J Cass Mason. When he arrived in Vicksburg a few weeks before, he met the chief quartermaster of the Mississippi, Colonel Ruben Heath. Heath told Mason that the Federal Government was offering to pay $5 per enlisted man and $10 per officer to any steamboat operator who would take them back to the north. Heath and Mason saw there was money to be made.

MORE PROBLEMS

Whenever the boat passed other vessels or sights of interest on its journey, the people on board moved from side to side to see, causing the *Sultana* to list badly. The listing worsened when the heavy cargo of sugar was unloaded at Memphis. Then, a short distance on, the *Sultana* hit a strong current.

Huge paddle steamers were a common sight on the Mississippi.

EXPLOSION

The patched starboard boiler could no longer take the pressure. It blew up and two other boilers followed suit. The blast tore out the centre of the vessel, ripping apart the upper decks. Both the sick bay and the officers' quarters were destroyed. One of the huge smoke stacks came crashing down and fire broke out.

ESCAPE

Those on deck flung whatever would float overboard and jumped in. Others lowered themselves into the water with ropes, but many were too weak to swim. They drowned in the river. One quick-thinking soldier saved himself on a makeshift raft made from the crate of Captain Mason's alligator. He bayonetted the alligator before climbing on board.

RESCUE

Some 200 of the 786 rescued would die later in hospital. The death toll made this the worst marine disaster in American history. However, the story of the *Sultana* was relegated to the back pages of the nation's newspapers. The day before, John Wilkes Booth, the man who assassinated Abraham Lincoln, had been cornered and killed. The public was more interested in the hunt for other conspirators than in this shipwreck.

WHY DID IT HAPPEN?

Maritime experts concluded that a number of things had contributed to the disaster. The boilers were badly designed – when the *Sultana* listed, the water in her boilers flowed out of one and flooded another. The ship's poor condition was also to blame, as was a lack of ballast, which, with the overloading, caused her to be top-heavy. Four men were deemed responsible for the overcrowding, including Colonel Heath, but since he left the army soon after the disaster, he never faced a military court.

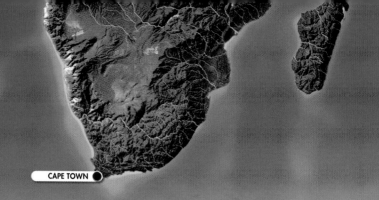

CAPE TOWN

HMS *Birkenhead*, 1852

On the evening of 25 February 1852, the British troopship *Birkenhead*, an iron paddle steamer, left Simon's Town, near Cape Town in South Africa, on the last leg of her voyage from Ireland to the Eastern Cape. On board were more than 600 people, mostly military personnel, but there were also paying passengers, including women and children.

DANGER POINT

The *Birkenhead* had to pass the rocks and shoals of Danger Point. The captain, Robert Salmond, had plotted a course that missed the point by almost 5 km (3 miles). Maybe it was because of strong currents or a compass error, but the *Birkenhead* drove directly onto the rocks. Captain Salmond was below when the hull was ripped open.

LIFEBOATS

There were only eight lifeboats – enough to carry 200 of the 600 aboard. However, only three of the eight were lowered successfully. The most senior officer on board, Lieutenant-Colonel Alexander Seton, a 37-year-old Scot, took charge of the troops. He drew his men around him and stressed the importance of maintaining discipline. It was at this point that the tradition of 'women and children first' was established.

SWIM FOR YOUR LIVES

Captain Salmond ordered that the engines be used to drag the ship off the rocks. This only made the damage worse. It became clear that the *Birkenhead* was going down. The captain shouted to the men to jump over the side to save their own lives, but Lieutenant-Colonel Seton drew his sword and stopped them. 'Stand fast,' he said. 'I beg you, do not rush the boats carrying the women and children. You will swamp them.'

British soldiers start the tradition of 'women and children first' and prepare to go down with the ship.

HONOURABLE MEN

Only three men disobeyed his orders. The rest held their ranks until, minutes later, the *Birkenhead* broke her back and disappeared under the waves. Many drowned and sharks killed more. Only 193 survived.

EYEWITNESS

A survivor, Captain Wright, wrote afterwards: 'The order and regularity that prevailed on board, from the time the ship struck until she totally disappeared, far exceeded anything that I thought could be effected... Everyone did as he was directed, and there was not a murmur or a cry amongst them until the ship made her final plunge.'

Kursk, 2000

On 12 August 2000, the huge Russian nuclear submarine *Kursk* was on naval exercises in the Barents Sea. She was the finest submarine in the Russian fleet, fitted with cutting-edge technology, and manned by a highly trained crew. Suddenly, there were two explosions on board. She sank with 118 crewmen on board.

ALIVE

A note found later on the body of 27-year-old Lieutenant-Captain Dmitri Kolesnikov revealed that some men survived the explosions, although they perished later. One sailor prevented a nuclear disaster by shutting down the two nuclear reactors that powered the submarine. Another 23 shut themselves into Compartment 9 at the far end of the sub.

RUMOURS

As news of the sinking of the submarine spread, it caused an international storm. At first, there were accusations that the *Kursk* had been sunk by a foreign submarine. There were also reports of communication with survivors. Both claims were untrue.

RESCUE ATTEMPTS

After two failed Russian attempts to save the trapped submariners, on 16 August the Russians requested British and Norwegian help. On 21 August Norwegian divers managed to open the submarine's external hatch, but they found no sign of life.

The crew of the Kursk stand to attention for a Navy Day parade before the tragedy.

RAISING THE KURSK

The following year, the *Kursk* was lifted from the sea floor. By the end of March 2002, the bodies of 115 crewmen had been found and identified.

A government investigation concluded that a training torpedo had exploded before lauching, blowing a hole in the hull. Heat from the blast and fire caused the other torpedoes to explode.

EYEWITNESS

In Dmitri Kolesnikov's note to his young wife, he had written down the names of the 23 crew with him in Compartment 9. The note read: 'It's too dark to write here, but I'll try by feel. It seems that there are no chances – maybe ten to twenty per cent. Let's hope that at least someone will read this... Regards to everybody. No need to be desperate.' A postmortem established that he died from carbon monoxide poisoning.

DAKAR

ZIGUINCHOR

MV *Le Joola*, 2002

On 29 August 2002, the ferry *Le Joola* was travelling to Dakar in Senegal. During a storm, all the passengers raced to one side of the overcrowded ferry to take cover, causing it to capsize. A reported 2,000 passengers were on board with at least 1,863 confirmed dead. It was Africa's worst maritime disaster.

OVERLOADED

Le Joola was built to carry a maximum of 600 people but that day at least 500 were crowded onto the top deck alone for the 16-hour journey from Ziguinchor to Dakar. As it was the low season for tourists, there were few cars in the ferry's hold to help stabilize it.

STORM

As the ferry rode into a storm, the people on the top deck on the starboard side were battered with wind and rain. When they moved to the port side for cover it unbalanced the ferry and the ship turned over. Although as a coastal ferry *Le Joola* was not supposed to sail further than six hours' sailing time from shore, she was 11 hours from shore when she capsized.

NATIONAL DISASTER

Senegal's president declared three days of national mourning and an official said: 'Senegal is only a small country. More than a thousand people died, and everyone knows someone who knows someone. We are all affected by something like this.'

Le Joola *was a roll-on, roll-off ferry, like the* Estonia.

RESPONSIBLE

Le Joola was a state-run ferry. President Abdoulaye Wade acknowledged his government's responsibility for the disaster and his transport and armed forces ministers resigned. A report concluded that overloading and negligence on the part of the operators and the Senegalese navy and rescue services were to blame.

 ## EYEWITNESS

Idrissa Diallo was in the US when he heard that his children had been killed. Their bodies were never recovered. 'A father who loses all his children, all of them... it has been very difficult. Every day they come back into my head... I feel traumatized whenever their birthdays are here because I wish I could celebrate with them.... But no... they are gone because of the recklessness and negligence of some government officials.'

Looking to the Future

Despite lessons being learned from every major shipwreck, there will always be risks at sea. After the *Titanic* disaster in 1912, an international treaty was drawn up to address maritime safety. It was called SOLAS (Safety Of Life At Sea), and it is still the most important treaty in force.

SOLAS

The SOLAS treaty has been updated regularly since its adoption in 1914. It sets the rules on safety equipment and procedures at sea. All shipping companies and mariners must follow the rules set out in the treaty.

A quick response from a well-equipped and well-rehearsed coast guard can save many lives.

OIL SPILLS

In 1978, the *Amoco Cadiz* oil tanker ran aground off the coast of Brittany. She split in two in bad weather and spilled her entire load of more than 1.6 million barrels of crude oil into the sea. Since then, new regulations have been adopted covering the design and construction of oil tankers and the transportation of hazardous cargo.

QUICK RESPONSE

In 1999, a Global Maritime Distress and Safety System became operational. This means that if a ship is in distress anywhere in the world, it is almost guaranteed assistance. Even if the crew has no time to radio for help, a distress message is transmitted automatically. Air-sea rescue helicopters can be mobilized to help.

CAPTAIN AND CREW

Despite new regulations, modern-day technology and safety precautions, the prevention of accidents and environmental damage still largely depends on the ability and experience of the ship's crew. In a crisis, it is vital that they react quickly and professionally, and put the safety of their passengers above commercial considerations.

IMO

The International Maritime Organization (IMO) is a United Nations agency established in 1948. It has responsibility for the safety and security of shipping. Its first task was to update the SOLAS treaty to make sea travel even safer. Over the decades it has had new problems to address, including that of oil spills and other pollution. Challenges of the future include the increase in modern piracy, especially off the African coast of Somalia, and the protection of the environment.

Timeline

19 July 1545, *Mary Rose*, Portsmouth England
The pride of King Henry VIII's fleet, the *Mary Rose* went out to greet an attacking French fleet and sank after listing badly as she turned.

25 February 1852, *Birkenhead*, Danger Point, South Africa
After running aground on rocks, soldiers on the *Birkenhead* stood back to allow the women and children to take the few lifeboats.

27 April 1865, *Sultana*, Mississippi River, USA
This steamship, carrying home prisoners-of-war after the American Civil War, was travelling up the Mississippi when her boilers blew up. Many were too weak to save themselves.

15 April 1912, *Titanic*, Atlantic Ocean, near Canada
The famous *Titanic* set off on her maiden transatlantic voyage. She sank after hitting an iceberg off the coast of Newfoundland. Of the 2,224 people on board, 1,519 people died.

29 May 1914, *Empress of Ireland*, St Lawrence River, Canada
The *Empress* collided with a Norwegian coal ship in thick fog on the St Lawrence River. Over 1,000 people lost their lives.

24 July 1915, *Eastland*, Chicago River, USA
At her mooring in Chicago, this unstable excursion steamer capsized as passengers boarded, killing 844 people.

6 December 1917, *Mont Blanc*, Halifax, Canada
Loaded with explosives, the *Mont Blanc* blew up in the harbour, devastating the area.

26 July 1956, *Andrea Doria*, Nantucket, USA
The Italian passenger ship, *Andrea Doria*, and the Swedish cruise ship, *Stockholm*, were involved in the worst liner collision in history.

21 December 1987, *Doña Paz*, Philippines
This overcrowded passenger ferry was hit by the unseaworthy oil tanker, *Vector*. Both ships and the surrounding sea burst into flames and up to 4,000 people are thought to have perished.

28 September 1994, *Estonia*, Baltic Sea
Halfway into its journey from Estonia to Sweden across the freezing and turbulent Baltic Sea, the *Estonia*'s bow door sheared off and water rushed in. Only 137 of the 989 passengers survived.

12 August 2000, *Kursk*, Barents Sea, Russia
Torpedo explosions on this Russian nuclear submarine during naval exercises caused the *Kursk* to sink. None of the crew survived.

29 August 2002, *Le Joola*, Senegal, West Africa
A passenger ferry overloaded and poorly maintained sank in bad weather off the coast of West Africa. At least 1,863 were confirmed dead – the worst African maritime disaster.

3 February 2006, *Al-Salam Boccaccio 98*, Red Sea
While the crew were trying to put out a persistent fire on board, the seawater that was used made the ferry capsize, causing over 1,000 deaths.

21 June 2008, *Princess of the Stars*, Philippines
Victim of Typhoon Fengshen, the *Princess of the Stars* capsized in brutal winds and high waves, causing nearly 800 deaths.

Glossary

aft the back end of a vessel

archipelago a group of islands

ballast any heavy material that provides stability or weight to a ship, especially one not carrying cargo

battery a group of weapons that can be used together in warfare

bow the front end of a vessel

broadside the firing of all weapons on one side of a warship

buoyancy the ability to float

capsize to turn over in water

diligence careful consideration

galley a type of ship powered by oars, commonly used as a warship in ancient and medieval times

HMS a Royal Navy ship prefix that means Her/His Majesty's Ship

hypothermia when a person's body temperature drops dangerously low due to extreme cold

kerosene also known as paraffin, kerosene is a type of fuel used for heating and to run some small engines

knots a unit of speed used for all vessels, equivalent to 1.85 kph (1.15 mph) on land

leeward the side of a ship that is sheltered from the wind

list to tip over at an angle

mariner another name for a sailor

maritime related to the sea

MS a ship's prefix that means Motor Ship

MV a ship's prefix that means Motor Vessel

premonition foreseeing something that happens in the future

RMS a ship's prefix that means Royal Mail Ship, indicating that it carries British mail

roll-on, roll-off (ro-ro) ferry a ferry that takes passengers and vehicles, with doors in the bow (at the front) and aft (at the back) to allow vehicles to drive on and off

shoals an area of shallow, rocky water, where rocks are often only visible at low tide

SS a ship's prefix that means Steamship

stern the rear of a ship

submariner a crewmember on a submarine

treaty a formal agreement between two or more countries

typhoon the name given to severe tropical storms in the Pacific, with winds of over 118 kph (73 mph)

Further Information

FURTHER READING

100 Things You Should Know About Shipwrecks, by Fiona MacDonald (Miles Kelly, 2010)

Eye Witness: Titanic, by Simon Adams (Dorling Kindersley, 2004)

Shipwreck Detective, by Richard Platt and Duncan Cameron (Dorling Kindersley, 2006)

Shipwrecks: Exploring Sunken Cities Beneath The Sea, by Mary M Cerullo (Dutton Books, 2009)

The 10 Most Unforgettable Shipwrecks, by Anita Griffith (Children's Press, 2008)

WEBSITES

National Geographic Channel
natgeotv.com/uk/shipwreck-graveyard

Ship Facts
www.theshipslist.com

Titanic Film Facts
www.titanicmovie.com/menu.html

Index